Exploring the Universe

The Moon

Susan Glass

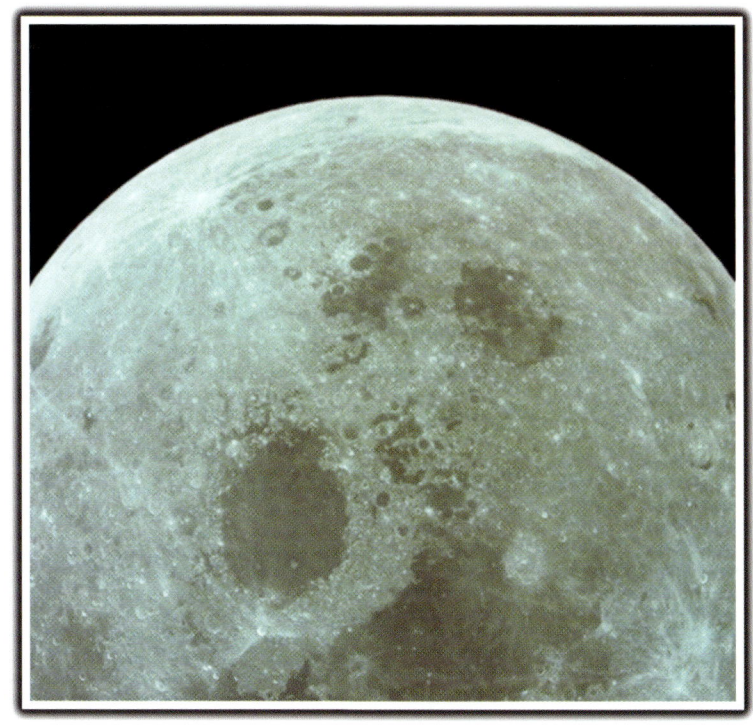

PERFECTION LEARNING®

Editorial Director: Susan C. Thies
Editor: Mary L. Bush
Design Director: Randy Messer
Book Design: Emily J. Greazel
Cover Design: Michael A. Aspengren

A special thanks to the following for his scientific review of the book: Kristin Mandsager, Instructor of Physics and Astronomy, North Iowa Area Community College

Image Credits:
©Associated Press: p. 19; ©Jeff Vanuga/CORBIS: p. 8; ©Roger Ressmeyer/CORBIS: p. 16 (top); ©Bettmann/CORBIS: p. 18 (left)

©ImageState Royalty Free: p. 12; Corel Professional Photos: back cover, front cover (background), pp. 5, 11 (dime), 17, 18 (right), 20, 22, 23; Perfection Learning: pp. 9, 10, 14, 16 (bottom); Photos.com: front cover (bottom left, middle, right), pp. 4, 7, 11 (quarter), 13, 15, 24

Text © 2006 by Perfection Learning® Corporation.
All rights reserved. No part of this book may be reproduced, stored in a retrieval system, or transmitted in any form or by any means, electronic, mechanical, photocopying, recording, or otherwise, without prior permission of the publisher. Printed in the United States of America.
For information, contact

Perfection Learning® Corporation
1000 North Second Avenue, P.O. Box 500
Logan, Iowa 51546-0500.
Phone: 1-800-831-4190
Fax: 1-800-543-2745
perfectionlearning.com

1 2 3 4 5 6 PP 10 09 08 07 06 05

Paperback ISBN 0-7891-6621-6
Reinforced Library Binding ISBN 0-7569-4646-8

Contents

1. Meet the Moon 4
2. What's It Like There? 6
3. Moon Movement 10
4. It's Just a Phase 13
5. Journey to the Moon 17

Internet Connections and
Related Reading for the Moon 20
Glossary 22
Index 24

Meet the Moon

Have you ever wondered about the Moon? How far away is it? How big is it? Why does it keep changing shape? Is there really a man on the Moon?

Scientists have answered many of these questions and others. Let's learn what they've discovered about the Moon.

What Is a Moon?

A **moon** is a large body that **revolves** around a planet. Earth is not the only planet with a moon. Most of the planets that **orbit** around the Sun have moons. Mercury and Venus are the only two planets with no known moons.

A Moon Memo

A moon is any of the 94 known bodies that orbit planets in the Solar System. The Moon (capitalized) is usually used when talking about the Earth's Moon.

The Earth's Only Moon

The Moon is Earth's only natural **satellite**. A satellite is an object that orbits around another object. Many human-made satellites circle the Earth. They bring you TV shows, weather forecasts, and directions in your car. But there is only one satellite that was put there by nature—the Moon.

How was the Moon formed? Most scientists now believe that the Moon was created when a large body in space collided with Earth. Pieces from both bodies stayed in space. Over time, gravity pulled this material together to form the Moon. This theory of the Moon's formation has been supported by rocks found on the Moon that are similar to rocks found on Earth.

Big and Far

Most planets have moons that are much smaller than they are. The Earth's Moon, however, is about one-fourth the size of Earth. It is about 2160 miles wide.

The Moon is the Earth's closest neighbor in space. Today, it is about 240,000 miles away. That's a long trip to visit a neighbor!

2 What's It Like There?

Imagine zooming to the Moon for a visit. What would you find there? The light, land, air, weather, and **gravity** on the Moon are much different than they are on Earth.

Can I Borrow Your Light?

Is there light on the Moon? Yes, thanks to the Sun. The Moon doesn't have its own light. It **reflects** light from the Sun. Moonlight is actually sunlight that bounces off the Moon.

As the Moon orbits the Earth, only the half facing the Sun is struck by sunlight. Any particular point on the surface of the Moon receives sunlight for about two weeks and is then dark for two weeks.

Where's the Air?

Earth has a blanket of air around it called an **atmosphere**. Earth's atmosphere contains a mixture of gases. One of these gases is the oxygen that your body needs to live.

The Moon doesn't have an atmosphere. The lack of air has several effects. Plants need carbon dioxide to make food. Animals need oxygen to breathe. Without either of these gases, no life can exist on the Moon.

Sunlight contains all the colors of the rainbow. On Earth, tiny particles of gas in the air scatter the blue light from the Sun. This makes the sky look blue. But the Moon has no air to scatter light particles, so the sky looks black.

Earth's atmosphere also protects us from extreme temperatures. But on the Moon, temperatures on the side facing the Sun are extremely hot, while temperatures on the other side are extremely cold.

No air also means that sounds can't be heard. Sound waves need something to travel through. Without air, sound waves cannot go anywhere.

The lack of atmosphere on the Moon also means there's no weather. Without rain, snow, or wind to cause **erosion**, very little changes on the Moon's surface.

What's on the Surface?

Most of the Moon is covered with rocks and dust. There are mountains and lowlands but no oceans or seas.

The mountain areas on the Moon are called *highlands*. These highlands are covered with light-colored rock.

Flat parts of the Moon's surface formed from cooled **lava**. From Earth, these areas look dark. Long ago, people saw these dark, flat areas and thought they were seas. The name stuck. Today these areas are still called *seas*. The Sea of Tranquillity, Sea of Showers, and Sea of Clouds are a few of the "seas" on the Moon.

The Man on the Moon

Have you heard stories about "the man on the Moon"? The pattern of dark seas on the Moon's surface makes it look like a face to some people. Other people claim to see a woman, a rabbit, or a buffalo in the Moon. What do you see?

Much of the Moon is covered with craters. Craters are bowl-shaped dents in the ground. They're made when rocks from space hit the Moon. Because there's no water or wind to wear down or fill in the craters, they've remained unchanged for millions of years.

What About Gravity?

Gravity is the force of one object's pull on another. Earth's gravity pulls everything toward its center. This force is what keeps you on the ground and not floating in the air.

The Moon has gravity that pulls things toward it too. But the Moon is much smaller than Earth, so its force of gravity is weaker than Earth's. In fact, the Moon's gravity is one-sixth of the Earth's gravity.

Gravity also affects the weight of objects. Weight is a measure of gravity's pull on an object. The more of something there is, the greater gravity's pull on it is. So a bigger person weighs more than a smaller one. If you divide your weight on Earth by six, that will tell you how much you would weigh on the Moon.

I'm Attracted to You

Gravity is also what holds the Sun, Moon, Earth, and other planets in their **orbits**. Each body is attracted to the others around it. This keeps them in their paths around one another.

The Moon's gravity causes the **tides** on Earth. Tides are the daily rising and falling of ocean water. As the Earth **rotates**, one side of it is always closer to the Moon. The Moon's pull on the Earth is stronger at this point, so it pulls the water away from the Earth. This causes the water to flow on to the land as it is pulled toward the Moon. This is called *high tide*. On the side of the Earth farthest away from the Moon, high tide also occurs. On this side, the Moon's attraction is weaker. The water bulges outward away from the Moon. As the Earth rotates, the water returns to the ocean. This is called *low tide*.

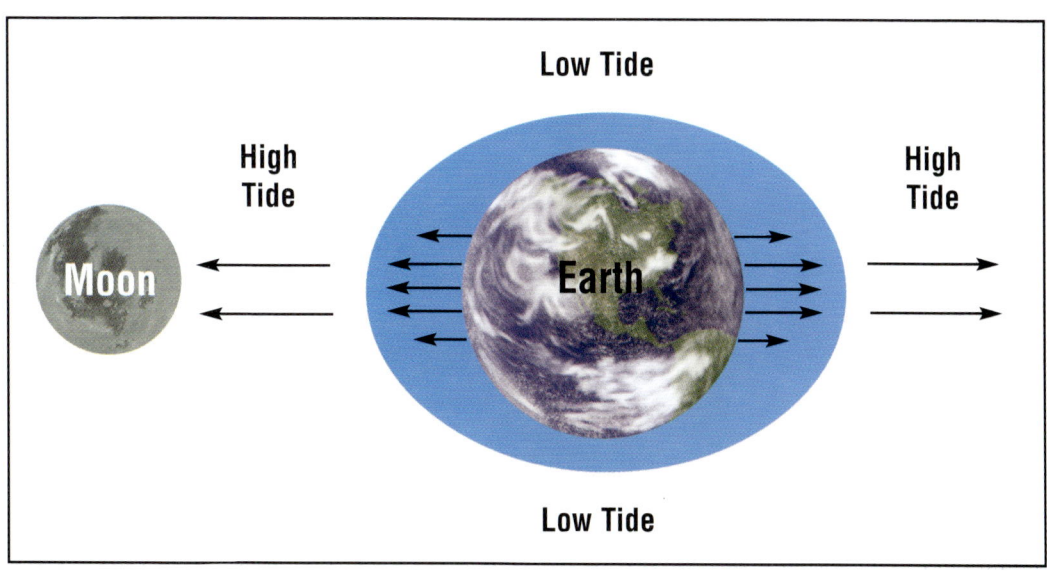

Moon Movement

Did you know that the word *month* comes from the word *Moon*? That's because it takes about a month for the Moon to make one orbit, or **revolution**, around the Earth. Every 27.3 days, the Moon completes one trip around the planet.

The Moon also rotates, or spins, on its **axis**. An axis is an imaginary line that runs through the center of the Moon. So while it's moving around the Earth, the Moon is also moving around its axis. That's a lot of Moon movement!

It's because of the Moon's rotation that we always see the same side of the Moon from Earth. The Moon rotates at the same speed as it revolves. This keeps the same side of the Moon facing the Earth at all times.

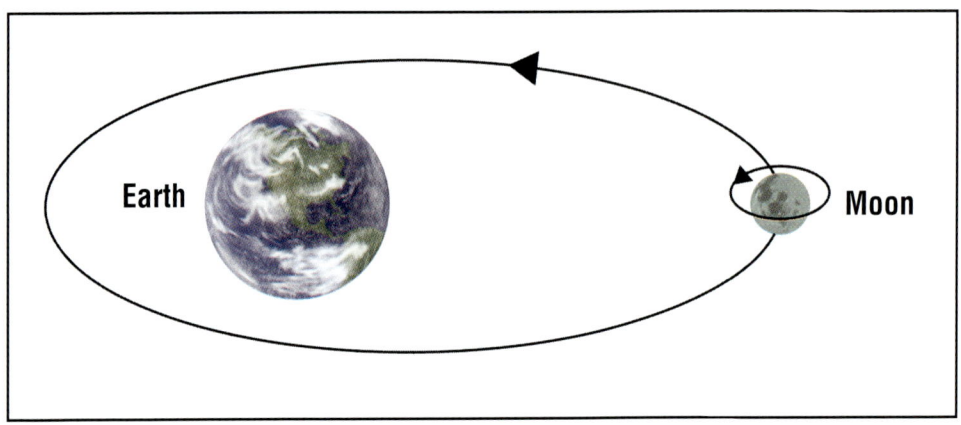

Inquire and Investigate: The Moon's Movement

Question: Does the Moon rotate as it revolves around the Earth?

Answer the question: I think the Moon _____ rotate.

Form a hypothesis: The Moon (does or does not) rotate as it revolves around the Earth.

Test the hypothesis:

Materials
- 9" × 11" piece of paper
- pencil
- 1 quarter
- 1 dime

Procedure
- Label each side of the paper with a direction (north, south, east, west).
- Place the quarter in the middle of the paper. This is the Earth.
- Place the dime on any side of the quarter with Roosevelt's nose pointing toward the quarter. The dime is the Moon. Note which direction the nose is pointing toward.
- Move the dime around the quarter so that the nose is always pointing toward the quarter. This represents the Moon's orbit around the Earth. Notice each time the nose points toward one of the directions. Make one complete revolution around the Earth. Did the nose point toward each of the directions during the revolution?

Observations: As the dime (Moon) revolved around the quarter (Earth), it faced each direction once.

Conclusions: The Moon rotates as it revolves around the Earth. If it didn't, the nose would have always pointed in the same direction. This rotation is why we always see the same side of the Moon from Earth.

What Do the Moon and a Merry-Go-Round Have in Common?

Both the Sun and the Moon appear to rise in the east, move across the sky, and then set in the west. But actually, neither the Sun nor Moon really "rises" or "sets." The Earth's movement just causes them to look as if they are moving. The Earth rotates once every 24 hours. As it turns, it makes the objects in the sky appear to move. It's like being on a merry-go-round. When you begin, the people waiting in line might be in front of you. As you turn, they move to the side and then behind you. But the people aren't really moving. Their position in relationship to you changes because *you're* moving. The same is true of the Earth and the Moon.

It's Just a Phase

One day the Moon looks like a banana. Another day it looks like a circle. Every day it looks fatter or thinner than the day before. Why does this happen?

The side of the Moon facing the Sun is always light. As the Moon orbits around the Earth, different parts of the lit Moon are visible. What part we see depends on the positions of the Moon, Earth, and Sun. The different parts or shapes of the Moon are known as the phases of the Moon.

PHASES OF THE MOON

New Moon

Waxing Crescent

First Quarter

Waxing Gibbous

Full Moon

Waning Gibbous

Last Quarter

Waning Crescent

The Phases of the Moon

When the Moon is on the same side of Earth as the Sun, the dark side of the Moon faces Earth. This means we can't see the Moon. This phase of the Moon's cycle is called the New Moon. It's called this because from this point on, it looks like a new Moon is forming.

For the next week, the Moon continues to move around the Earth. More of the lit Moon becomes visible. First it looks like a thin fingernail cutting. Then it begins to look like a banana. Each day the crescent shape gets a little wider. A week after the New Moon, the Moon is a half circle. This is called the First Quarter Moon. Why is it called a first "quarter" when it looks like a half? It's because the Moon is a quarter of the way through its cycle.

The Moon continues to grow larger throughout the next week. When it's more than a half circle but less than a whole circle, it's called a Gibbous Moon. *Gibbous* is from an old word that means "hunchback." The lit part of the Moon now has a hunchback.

A week after the First Quarter, the Moon is a full circle. This phase is the Full Moon.

Each day after the Full Moon, the Moon begins to thin out. It becomes a Gibbous Moon, then a Last (or Third) Quarter Moon, and finally a Crescent Moon. On the last day of the cycle, the Moon is once again a New Moon.

Waxing or Waning?

When the lit-up part of the Moon looks larger each day, it is said to be waxing. When it looks smaller each day, it is waning. There are Waxing Crescent and Gibbous Moons and Waning Crescent and Gibbous Moons.

Something to Think About

Did you notice that there's a difference of more than 2 days in the time the Moon completes a revolution around the Earth (27.3 days) and the time it takes for the Moon to complete its phases (29.5 days)? That's because the Earth is also revolving around the Sun (taking the Moon with it). Every month, the Earth moves $1/12$ of the way around the Sun. This movement affects the time it takes for the Moon to go through its phases. Each time, the Moon has to travel a bit farther around the Earth to get "full" again.

Lunar Eclipses

A **lunar eclipse** occurs when the Sun, Earth, and Moon are in a position where the Earth blocks the Sun from the Moon. When this happens, Earth's **shadow** falls on the Moon. The Moon is dark but can appear gray, brown, red, or orange. A lunar eclipse can only take place during the Full Moon phase. However, only a few of these phases happen at the same time as the Moon passes through the Earth's shadow. This makes a lunar eclipse a rare sight.

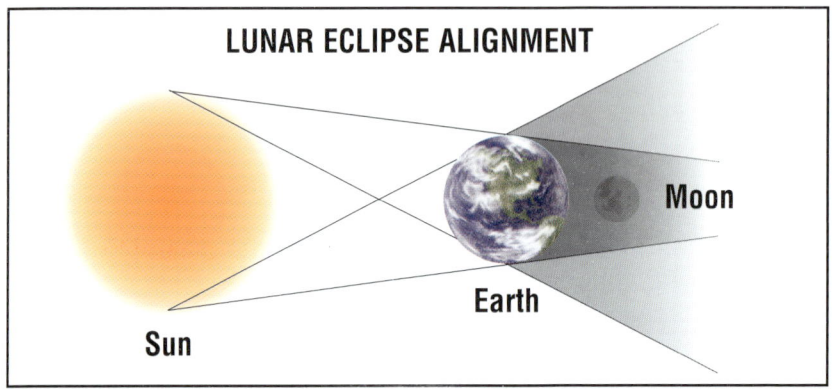

Journey to the Moon

For thousands of years, people have been looking at the Moon and wondering what was up there. For hundreds of years, scientists have been studying the Moon through telescopes. Then in 1959, the Soviet Union sent the first **unmanned** spacecraft to get a closer look. Five years later, the United States sent the unmanned Ranger 7 to explore the Moon. Other unmanned Moon missions followed. Pictures and information were collected so humans could later travel to the Moon.

To Go Where None Had Gone Before

In 1969, the United States launched Apollo 11 with three astronauts aboard. Neil Armstrong, Buzz Aldrin, and Michael Collins became the first men to visit the Moon. More Apollo missions followed. By 1972, twelve American astronauts had made it to the Moon.

Apollo 11 crew (left to right): Neil Armstrong, Michael Collins, Buzz Aldrin

Scientist of Significance

Neil Armstrong was born in 1930 in Wapakoneta, Ohio. He became a navy fighter pilot, then a test pilot, and finally an astronaut. In 1966, Armstrong piloted the Gemini 8 and docked it on another spacecraft in orbit. This was the first successful linking of two ships in space. In July of 1969, Armstrong became the first person to actually step foot on the Moon. When he did, he radioed these famous words back to Earth: "That's one small step for man, one giant leap for mankind."

The astronauts brought home information about the Moon. They found rocks and dust, but no water, plants, or little green men. They confirmed that there was no life on the Moon. The astronauts also planted an American flag, played golf, bounced around in moon buggies, and watched a beautiful **earthrise**. With no wind or water to erase them, the footprints the astronauts left on the Moon may last for millions of years.

Astronauts Armstrong and Aldrin left footprints in the Sea of Tranquillity during the Apollo II mission to the Moon.

Ice on the Moon?

In 1994, the unmanned Clementine spacecraft took photographs of the Moon's surface. These pictures showed that there might be ice at the Moon's south **pole**. Then in 1998, the United States sent the Lunar Prospector to orbit the Moon. The information it collected showed that there does appear to be some ice in the rocks at both the north and south poles of the Moon. The possible discovery of water may lead to future journeys to the Moon.

Technology Link

The Lunar Prospector was a small but effective spacecraft sent to study the Moon. The Prospector was only 4 feet tall and 4 1/2 feet wide. It was shaped like a short, fat drum.

The Prospector orbited the Moon and took photographs. These pictures were used to make better maps of the Moon's surface. The spacecraft also scanned the Moon for minerals and ice deposits near the Moon's poles. This information helps scientists piece together the history of the Moon.

The Lunar Prospector was never supposed to come home. It crashed into a crater when it ran out of fuel on July 31, 1999.

Internet Connections and Related Reading for the Moon

http://www.windows.ucar.edu/tour/link=/earth/moons_and_rings.html
Look through a "Window to the Universe" to get a clearer view of the Moon. Explore the frequently asked questions and information on lunar eclipses as well.

http://teacher.scholastic.com/researchtools/articlearchives/space/moon.htm
How big is the Moon? How old is it? An astronomer answers these and many other kids' questions about the Moon.

http://www.worldalmanacforkids.com/explore/space/moon.html
The *World Almanac for Kids* provides information on a variety of Moon topics.

http://www.enchantedlearning.com/subjects/astronomy/moon/phases.shtml
The colorful diagram and simple definitions at this site explain the phases of the Moon.

http://lunar.arc.nasa.gov/
Find out more about the Lunar Prospector and the Moon at this official NASA Web site.

Experiments with the Sun and Moon by Salvatore Tocci. This book presents projects and experiments that explore scientific principles related to the Sun and Moon, particularly those that explain eclipses. Crabtree Publishing, 2003. [RL 3.5 IL 3–5] (6873001 PB 6873006 HB)

Man on the Moon by Anastasia Suen. A picture book about the Apollo 11 mission that introduces space exploration, people, and historical events. Viking, 1997. [RL 2 IL 2–4] (5916406 HB)

The Moon by Paulette Bourgeois. A unique combination of facts, folklore, experiments, and activities explains scientific discoveries about the Moon. Kids Can Press, 1997. [RL 4.7 IL 2–4] (3217701 PB 3217702 CC)

Moon Walk by Dana Rau. When ten-year-old Tomas and his friends visit the National Air and Space Museum, they see the Apollo 11 Lunar Module, and suddenly Tomas finds that he has become Neil Armstrong as he makes his historic walk on the Moon in 1969. Soundprints, 2003. [RL 3 IL 1–4] (3644901 PB 3644902 CC)

The Moon Seems to Change by Franklyn M. Branley. Explains the phases of the Moon—the changes that seem to happen to it as it goes around the Earth. HarperCollins, 1987. [RL 2 IL 1–3] (8746301 PB 8746302 CC)

Moonwalk, the First Trip to the Moon by Judy Donnelly. All the thrills and danger of the first voyage to the Moon are described in an easy-to-read format. Random House, 1989. [RL 3 IL 2–4] (8957601 PB 8957602 CC)

What the Moon Is Like by Franklyn M. Branley. This completely revised and reillustrated edition tells young readers what we've learned about the Moon since the astronauts were there. HarperCollins, 1987. [RL 3 IL K–3] (8584701 PB 8584702 CC)

- RL = Reading Level
- IL = Interest Level

Perfection Learning's catalog numbers are included for your ordering convenience. PB indicates paperback. CC indicates Cover Craft. HB indicates hardback.

Glossary

atmosphere (AT muhs sfear) mixture of gases that surround a planet or other body in space

axis (AK sis) imaginary line around which an object turns

earthrise (ERTH reyez) the rising of the Earth above the Moon's horizon as seen from space or the Moon

erosion (uh ROH zhuhn) the movement of small pieces of rock and soil due to water, wind, or ice

gravity (GRAV uh tee) force of attraction between two bodies in space

lava (LAH vah) liquid rock from a volcano that rises above the surface

lunar eclipse (LOON er ee KLIPS) darkening of the Moon when the Earth blocks the Sun and casts its shadow on the Moon (see separate entry for *shadow*)

moon (moon) body that revolves around a planet (see separate entry for *revolve*)

orbit	(OR bit) to move around a body in space in a path controlled by the force of gravity (verb); path that a body in space follows around a larger body (noun) (see separate entry for *gravity*)
pole	(pohl) most northern and southern points on the Moon (or the Sun or a planet)
reflect	(ruh FLEKT) to bounce back toward the point where something began
revolution	(rev uh LOO shuhn) circular movement of one object around another
revolve	(ruh VAWLV) to move in a circular motion around an object
rotate	(ROH tayt) to spin around on an axis or fixed point (see separate entry for *axis*)
satellite	(SAT uh leyet) object that orbits another object (see separate entry for *orbit*)
shadow	(SHAD oh) dark shape on a surface that falls behind an object blocking a source of light
tide	(teyed) rise and fall of the ocean caused by the Moon's gravity (see separate entry for *gravity*)
unmanned	(uhn MAND) not having any people on board

23

Index

Aldrin, Buzz, 17
Armstrong, Neil, 17, 18
atmosphere, 6–7
Collins, Michael, 17
distance from Earth, 5
exploration of the Moon, 17–19
    Apollo 11, 17, 18
    Clementine, 19
    Lunar Prospector, 19
    Ranger 7, 17
formation of the Moon, 5
gravity, 8–9
light, 6

lunar eclipses, 16
phases, 13–15, 16
revolution, 5, 10, 11, 15
rotation, 10, 11
size, 5
sound, 7
surface, 7–8
    craters, 8
    highlands, 7
    seas, 7, 8
tides, 9
water (ice), 19
weather, 7